PRESSING TOWARD IT

Navoun Maxwell

ISBN 978-1-63903-262-4 (paperback)
ISBN 978-1-63903-263-1 (digital)

Christian Faith Publishing, Inc.
832 Park Avenue
Meadville, PA 16335
www.christianfaithpublishing.com

Printed in the United States of America

In MEMORY OF MY grandparents: the late bishop Willie Lee Maxwell, who transitioned into eternal life on January 9, 2015, and the late missionary mother Nancy Maxwell, who transitioned into eternal life on January 14, 2020

To my amazing mom, LaTiesha McCaskill, and my awesome father, Minister Robert McCaskill Sr.

I press towards the mark for the prize of the
high calling of God in Christ Jesus.

—Philippians 3:14

CONTENTS

INTRODUCTION

GRACE AND PEACE FROM God, our Father and our Lord, and our Savior, Jesus Christ! The Lord gave me this title in the year 2018 to encourage those that are going through the many obstacles we encounter in our daily lives. The Lord helped me to examine my own circumstances and trauma, and it is a proven fact that we all go through some form of trouble. We have goals, desires, and dreams that we want to pursue. You begin to plan the life that you want to live, and sometimes, we alter our choices to make our lives to be successful. We work hard to make our dreams livable, but then there are roadblocks that overshadow our desires. We begin to have negative vibes, and we decide to not focus on what God has put in us to do. The question is this: What do we do?

In the Christian perspective, what you are facing is called a process. Some of you are dealing with issues in your relationship or in your marriage. You and your spouse are trying to work out your obstacles to ignite the romance and passion. Some of you are trying to pursue goals, but the obstacle of sickness and other obstacles are in the way, and then you begin to say, "I can't do this anymore." You are in this race for a reason. Hebrews 12:1 states, "Wherefore seeing we also are compassed about with so great a cloud of witnesses, let us lay aside every weight, and the sin which doth so easily beset us, and let us run with patience the race that is set before us."

The Lord encouraged me to write this book to encourage those who do not know how to overcome obstacles and to press toward the mark.

I pray that this book would be a blessing and that it will change your life for the better in Jesus's name.

CHAPTER 1

WHAT IS TROUBLE?

Whether you are saved or not, everyone will experience trouble. When we think of trouble, we think of negative vibes that occur in our lives. Trouble is any situation that causes us to be disturbed. It causes us to become agitated. When we experience trouble, we expect a source to alter our situations. As Christians, when we hear about trouble, our immediate thought is this: "Yes, I'm exempt from trouble" or "Yes, I have a free pass because I belong to Christ."

Christians get enlivened that once we become saved, we have zero amount of trouble. It does not matter if you are a Christian or not; everyone will have to face trouble. The Bible says in Job 14:1 that "a man who is born of a woman is of a few days and full of trouble." I had that mindset when I was sixteen years old. At that age, I gave my life to the Lord, and that was the best decision I have ever made. As happy as I was about living for God, I was elated that I did not have to go through trouble because I belong to the Lord. Once I became saved and started living for God, I still endured trouble.

I grew up in a church where the seasoned mothers and saints of God would say that "trouble would come on every side." Everywhere you turn, there is trouble. Trouble in your home, in your marriage, in your relationships, in your school education, in your ministry, and even in your Christian life. We all will encounter trouble in every aspect of life. The Word of God says that we are troubled on every side but not distressed. The next thing that we must focus on is how to respond to our troubles.

CHAPTER 2

YOUR RESPONSE TO TROUBLE

In every walk of your life, all of us will experience trouble. Everywhere you look, there's trouble. We are not, and I repeat—*not*, exempt from trouble. It does not matter if you are saved or not; trouble will hit. The question is, How do you conquer trouble?

Facing challenges is not meant to harm you but to test your emotional mettle in an illness, unemployment, marriage and family, death, and heading on a new venture without a known future. Many of us feel that when trouble arises, God is punishing us. This is a public service announcement: *God is not punishing you.* Rather, facing challenges and obstacles as a punishment is how the Lord is testing your faith. Have you ever been in a church where they do testimony service, and when people are testifying, they express their emotions of who God is in the good days? One might say, "Well, in my good days, God is wonderful, awesome, and amazing." Another might add, "Oh, honey, days when I am well, he is all that. He's a great god, and I will forever praise him in the good times."

Well, is God good to you in the bad? When you realize that you are dealing with your obstacles that you yourself cannot come out of, what do you do then? Are you going to serve God and acknowledge him the same way you do in the good? Some of you are saying now, "I can't put my trust in God because I doubt that he is not going to handle it. This problem is too big for God to work on, and so I will handle." The Bible says that the disciples were on the boat, and there was a big storm; and while Jesus was sleeping, they were fearful of their lives and called on the Lord for help. Jesus woke up and commanded the storm to be in a place of peace. When the storm was settled, Jesus looked at his disciples and asked, "Where is your faith?"

These are the questions that the Lord is asking you: "If you can believe in me in the good days, why not believe me in the bad? If you can praise me and worship me during the good, then why not do the same when facing trouble?" It does not matter to God if the problem is big or small. I serve a notice to everyone who is reading this book: God is God, and he can do anything except fail. God is not punishing you but is testing your faith. Whenever I dealt with trouble—and believe me, I had a lot—my grandmother, Missionary/Mother Nancy Maxwell, always said to me, "Nay, what do I always tell you? What is my favorite scripture? In thee, O Lord, do I put my trust."

People will walk away from you and will refuse to help you. You do not have a source to depend on, and that is the reason you are feeling depressed. Some of you are saying right now, "I don't have anyone to lean on. Those who I classified as my friends abandoned me when my trouble escalated. My family will not succor my every need." You need to understand that Jesus is the source of your strength, and he will be the only one to *never* fail you. Jesus is the same yesterday, today, and forever more so justifies that if the Lord is a great god in the good, then we can conclude that he is a great god in the bad.

Trouble, whether it is big or small, will take a toll on all of us. From a psychological perspective, stress and anxiety will take the absolute lead once any level of trouble is marinated. Stress and anxiety will then lead to something more serious, such as health-related conditions, which consist of a heart attack, panic attacks, or even a stroke. In a mental and emotional state, you are not prepared nor are you ready to receive the unexpected. Keep in mind that trouble is circulating all around us. Don't let your troubles overtake you; you overtake them. You take full control of your situations and command peace to settle in. The glory of the Lord wants to settle in your life, and it is up to you to receive his glory to rest in your troubles.

The Bible says in Acts chapter 2 that you shall receive power after the Holy Ghost has come upon you. The key word in that scripture verse is *power*. Sometimes, we surmise that the power the apostle

Peter is referring to is speaking in tongues. No, no, no. Those who are reading this part, pay close attention. You have the power to control your circumstances. It is up to you to take it by force. We are not violent people, but we are violent intercessors and prayer warriors, wrestling not against flesh and blood, but against principalities and powers of this evil world. Be the force to tell your sickness not to mess with you from accomplishing your goals. Be the force to demand your enemies that they can't mess with you, your family, your children, your husband, your wife, your pastor, your ministry, and your church family. Tell those who talked about you, lied to you, and have forgotten about you that they can't ruin your life because you belong to the Lord. It is in him that you move, that you live, and that you have your well-being. Command yourself this: *I will be prosperous!* Gain total access to victory.

When I was in high school, I took a course entitled Honors Algebra 2, and in that course, the topic of equations and formulas were mentioned. One of the formulas I studied was the Pythagorean theorem, which says a2 + b2 = c2. If we add a2 and b2, then we will get c2. Plain and simple. When you are dealing with any kind of trouble, I want you to use this formula because it will alter your life.

Pain Formula: Pain + Praise = Power

When you encounter pain (physical, emotional, and mental) and allow your trust in the Lord to activate, that will produce your praise. Pain and praise combined will give you power. The apostle Paul said in 2 Corinthians 10:4 that "the weapons we fight with are not the weapons of this world. On the contrary, they have divine power to demolish strongholds." When you realize that your back is against the wall, you don't fight with your fist or with guns, but you fight with your praise. Don't ever allow anyone to stop you from praising God because what you are doing is knocking the devil out with your praise. This is why the Scripture says that the devil is under our feet.

Any form of sickness, messed-up marriages and relationships, addictions, and judgmental church folks are your opponent, and if you want to gain access to victory, then you have to give God a praise that says he is God, and God alone can fight your battles. Don't be afraid of your circumstances. God didn't give us the spirit of fear but of power, love, and of a sound mind. If you want to see a change in your life, then you know what you have to do. You answered right: *Put a praise on it.*

Show the enemy that he is a liar and that you are nothing to play with. Tell your troubles this: "Don't start none, won't be none." It is something about praising your Yahweh. Growing up, the seasoned saints would sing the song "When Praises Go Up, Blessings Come Down." You will feel a lot better when you begin to praise the Lord. The scripture says, "They that wait upon the Lord shall renew their strength" (Isaiah 40:31 KJV). While you are waiting on the Lord, praise him and worship him during the wait. It's more than just waiting, but it's what you do in the waiting process. Your praise and worship produce strength and power from the Holy Ghost. Use that power to see a change in your life.

CHAPTER 3

FAITH: ACTIVATING YOUR FAITH

In the life of a Christian believer, faith is an important tool to carry as you walk and explore this Christian path with the Lord. According to the New International Version, Hebrews 11:1 states, "Now faith is confidence in what we hope for and assurance about what we do not see." Whenever you deal with trouble in your life, you need to know how to respond to them in the spiritual realm. When you are in a situation that might be too complicated for you to control, it is imperative that you become spiritually minded. It is not easy going through so many tests and trials. Sometimes, when you are at that level, you begin to find people in your life who will be willing to be there for you in your time of need. Let me give you a public service announcement: *Not everyone will be there to support you and comfort you.* Read that again.

You will have those who will stab you in the back and bring harm to you. Others will act like they support you, but they are going around telling your business to others to make you become both the headlines and the inside story. Be careful of who you allow to come in your circle of life. Use your spirit of discernment to discern who's for you and who's against you. When we are in that environment, we become more and more stressed; and from a psychological perspective, it is not good to be in that state of mind. Have you ever asked yourself, "Who can I talk to that will always be there for me?" I want to encourage every reader that you are *not* alone. Let me reiterate that statement again: *You are not alone!* Why? I'm glad you asked. You are not alone because you have Jesus. David said, "The Lord is my shepherd, and I shall not want" (Psalm 23:1). You should never have someone who will say they're here for you, then the next day, they turn away from you. You have God because he made a promise never to leave you or forsake you.

When I was in middle school, I would read a poster in the cafeteria that said "Got milk?" I want to ask you one question: "Got God?" When you are alone, you can always collogue with him. You can tell him all the things that's holding you back from pressing toward your destiny. Know that God is always present while you're going through. Let us go into the scene when Peter was walking on water and was doubting the Lord. This is what Matthew 14:24–31 says:

> But the ship was now in the midst of the sea, tossed with waves: for the wind was contrary.
>
> And in the fourth watch of the night Jesus went unto them, walking on the sea.
>
> And when the disciples saw him walking on the sea, they were troubled, saying, it is a spirit: and they cried out for fear.
>
> But straightway Jesus spoke unto them, saying, Be of good cheer; it is I; be not afraid.
>
> And Peter answered him and said, Lord, if it be thou, bid me to come unto thee on the water.
>
> And he said, Come. And when Peter came down out of the ship, he walked on the water to go to Jesus.
>
> But when he saw the wind boisterous, he was afraid, and beginning to sink, he cried, saying, Lord, save me.
>
> And immediately, Jesus stretched forth his hand and caught him, and said unto him, O thou of little faith, wherefore didst thou doubt?

When we embarked in the year 2020, we stepped into a new year, but also a new decade. In 2019, many people prophesied that

2020 will become a great year for us and that we will experience twenty-twenty vision. However, our understanding of what 2020 will bring was altered due to the COVID-19 pandemic. The year 2020 will be marked in history as one of the most momentous years we've encountered in our lives and as a nation. Everything that we were adapted to for a long time has shifted. Schools have closed, and academic learning is displayed online. Churches were shut down, and many clergy leaders transitioned to virtual services. Because of the number of death cases in the US and all parts of the world, people are becoming more fearful.

In 2020, we've also experienced racism and hate crimes in our nation. The tragic death of the late George Floyd and the late Breonna Taylor led to both a national and international protest. More hate crimes and attempted murders among African Americans led to more protest marches and riots. We are in 2021, and people are still fearful. In this season, we should not be fearful and doubt the Lord. Timothy stated, "For God has not given us a spirit of fear, but of power and of love and of a sound mind" (2 Timothy 1:7). This is not the hour to doubt the Lord but to activate your faith. Just because this issue is greater than others, are you going to take this opportunity to trust God less?

My grandmother, the late Missionary Mother Maxwell loved reciting this psalm of David: "In thee, o Lord, do I put my trust; let me never be ashamed: deliver me in thy righteousness" (Psalm 31:1). Don't doubt the Lord. You begin to doubt him when you have a flashback of previous encounters that you couldn't handle, and you compare one to the other. David said that some trust in horses and others in chariots, but we shall trust in the name of the Lord. When you put your faith in God, you will realize that what you thought was impossible, God can make it possible, and it is all because you believed in him. You have to make a consensus decision to believe in the report of the Lord.

It is imperative for all my great readers to know what activated faith is and how to activate it. Activated faith is performing what was declared over your life with confidence. When you act in faith, it shows that you fully trust in God's word. God never fails, and he knows exactly what he is doing. Jesus said that we should not fear, but only believe. Your faith is activated when you first believe. Let's revisit the scene with Peter walking on water. If he activated his faith and not doubt, then he could have walked on water without ever sinking. Take a look at Hebrews 11 where you will find great biblical leaders who procured prosperity using their faith. When you activate your faith, you will see the manifestation of God in any area of your life. Whether it is finding employment, getting a new house or car, or even reestablishing a relationship, you will see God's hand at work.

The apostle James gives an outline of activated faith precisely. The Bible says, "For as the body without the spirit is dead, so faith without works is dead also" (James 2:27). I want to break this verse down with you and for you. The apostle James wants to encourage everyone that you need more than faith to see the glory of God moving in your life. You can't just pray for the Lord to do something in your life, say you have faith, and that's the end of it. That alone is not enough, but you need to do your part.

Take a look at this example. A high school student named Danny is preparing for a math exam in five days, and he doesn't comprehend half of the material that will be on the exam. He surmises that he will utterly fail and decides to give up. Danny's mother comes into the room, discerning that he is feeling depressed, and encourages him to seek the Lord and have faith. He does just that, and that's the end of it. If Danny had faith, believed that God will give him the understanding he needs while studying, then he will do well on the exam. This puts you in the mind of Solomon. When King David was close to death, he passed the torch of being the next anointed king to his younger son, Solomon. Solomon had a difficult time understanding the laws of the land and to apply which law to use for a legal case. He then asked the Lord for wisdom, and while asking the Lord for wisdom, he continued to study more. When it was time to handle the first case, I'm positive that Solomon was nervous, but he didn't doubt the Lord and believed that his request was granted to him. Because he activated his faith, Solomon became the wisest man in the kingdom.

In this hour, this is not the moment to give up. This is not the time to give in to the flesh and allow the flesh to take over your mind. You need to tell the flesh to back up and to put on the spirit man. You need to become spiritually minded and command yourself that you trust in God. God doesn't want you to give up. The apostle Paul said, "And let us not be weary in doing well in due season, we shall reap, if we faint not" (Galatians 6:9). You can't reap your harvest if you decide to give up. When you activate your faith, you will then produce. You will see your marriage or relationship restored because you activated your faith. You will experience healing taking place because you activated your faith. Apostle Peter said, "By his stripes, ye are healed" (1 Peter 2:24).

Healing can be physically, mentally, emotionally, and spiritually. Because you put your trust in the Lord, your body will be healed. Broken marriages and relationships will be healed. Minds will be altered. You need to produce and show the devil that he tried to harm you and mess with your mind, but his plan didn't work. You need to declare to God, "I will put my faith in you and will forever trust your report." Activate your faith, believe God's word, and you will see a discrepancy in your life, whether in your business, your education, your family, your health, and even in your marriage. Get ready to be produced in the name of Jesus! Activate your faith, and watch God. Know that God loves you and wants you to have a prosperous life.

CHAPTER 4

FIERCE: ROAR LIKE A LION

Any trouble that we encounter will be very difficult to cope with. We can testify that we go through many traumas and triggers of the enemy, and as a result, we become more anxious, depressed, physically drained, emotionally drained, and mentally drained. From a psychological perspective, we begin to sometimes take things to the next level, such as being addicted to drugs, alcohol, food, video games, etc. Yes, this is a process you're in, but we sometimes give in to the devil's plans. We give up too easily and then allow the devil to take course in our lives. This is *not* the hour nor it is the season to allow the devil to become victorious. You have to be bold in the faith. In this chapter, you will learn how to be fierce and to be ready to stand your ground. All right, let's dive into this chapter. Let's go!

When you think of the word *fierce*, what pops in your head? If you answered *ferocious*, *aggressive*, *savage*, and *angry*, then you answered correctly. When you are fierce, your opponents fear you, and you will show your enemies that you are not the one to play with. Do you remember chapter 2 about the power of God? God has given you power for a reason. Along with the power of God, you also carry the anointing of God with you. Any traumas or triggers of the enemy that we face, we sometimes respond to the natural side. We cry, break dishes, and cuss, which will then lead to giving in to the devil's tactics and have him become victorious. It does not matter how big or small the problem may be, you must take it by force.

If you have a marriage that is on the verge of separation, do not give the devil that satisfaction to enter in and take control of your marriage. True marriage is all about covenant, and Satan abhors covenant. The devil will be like the plankton from *SpongeBob SquarePants* and will establish plans plus a motive to dismantle what God has put together. The devil will not stop until he is successful. The same applies with family trauma. You are trying to promote peace and unity among your family, but the devil is being messy and being sneaky. Satan is plotting to attack your health, and while your health is under attack, you then might experience a disorder in psychology, known as *psychosomatic disorder*. Psychosomatic disorder results from stress and anxiety due to major health issues such as high blood pressure, heart attack, stroke, cancer, sickle cell anemia, ulcers, etc. It is a mental health disease in which the body and the mind connects. I have had this mental disease before, and it is difficult to cope with, but with my faith in the Lord, I was able to overcome it.

Any situation that you encounter in your life, this is not the moment to give up. If you are at the point of giving up, then I understand the purpose. If you only knew how I responded naturally while dealing with my health issue and pain in my wounds, believe me, I wanted to give up. Let me share with you my testimony. I did not want to continue with my pain and suffering. I felt as though giving up was the only option. At a young age, I was diagnosed with sickle cell anemia, and being in the hospital every year made it difficult to continue in life.

In April 2017, I developed leg ulcers, and the pain from my ulcers messed with my mind. I do not know if you have been like this before, but I did not want to pray, go on a consecration, fast, and even go to church. I would read the scriptures, concur to every word, but I could not accept it. There was a time when I reached my maximum pain level, and I asked the Lord to let me die. I was depressed and had suicidal thoughts because I felt that the only way to become pain-free is death, but the Lord reminded me about endurance and patience. The Lord revealed to me that he will always be present while I am in the fire, just like how he was present when the three Hebrew men were inside the fiery furnace.

A great friend and elder in the Lord's church said to me, "Whenever you go through the fire, do not let your circumstances control you, but you control them." He proceeded to then tell me to push beyond the pain, push the frustration, and to push beyond the doubt. How do you push beyond the pain, the frustration, and the doubt? Push by praying and crying out to God. When you know that you are a child of God, you are righteous, and the righteous believers are heard when they cry out to the Lord. David said in Psalm 34:15 that "the eyes of the Lord are upon the righteous and his ears are open unto their cry."

In our life, there is trouble all around us, but when you are considered righteous in the eyes of the Lord, you will receive the benefits from the Lord God on how to overcome traumas and troubles. The benefits of handling circumstances are knowing that you are heard and delivered. In Psalm 34:17, David said, "The righteous cry, and the Lord heareth and delivereth them out of all their troubles." Any trouble that you endure, you will be delivered from. I want you to assert over your life that you are coming out of depression, anxiety, stagnation, failures, health conditions, and suicidal thoughts, and that you are entering into your deliverance in the name of the Lord Jesus Christ!

The next thing that we are going to dig into is using your mouth as your spiritual weapon against the enemy. The words in your mouth have total power. You will begin to witness the full manifestation of the power of God at work just by using your mouth. You will learn how to be fiercely bold and to roar like a lion. Lions are one of the most dangerous animals in the animal kingdom, and in addition, the roar of the lion is one of the most terrifying sounds in the kingdom. The purpose of a lion's loud roar is to scare off intruders and to show a sense of power. It is imperative to know that you need to be prepared for the plans of the devil, and by doing so, you need to embed the word of God into your spirit.

Timothy said to study the Word of God to show thyself approved (read 2 Timothy 2:15 KJV). This is a way to prepare yourself for battle, along with fasting and praying. The devil is irritated when we quote the word of the Lord because Hebrews 4:12 states, "For the word of God is quick, and powerful, and sharper than any two-edged sword, piercing even to the dividing asunder of soul and spirit, and of the joints and marrow, and is a discerner of the thoughts and intents of the heart." God's word is powerful, and when you declare the word of the Lord to sickness, pain, depression, etc., then those things will have to bow down at the name of Jesus and flee from you. The word of God dwells in you, and now you can be bold in the faith to withstand against the wiles of the devil. This is your moment where you take it by force to let the devil know that you are a weapon of power and declare with confidence the word of the Lord for your life.

In the book of Proverbs 28:1, it says, "The wicked flee when no one pursues, but the righteous are bold as a lion." Lions are not afraid of any intruders that come in the way to intervene and to destroy. Do not be afraid to roar at the face of your enemies. Any sickness, depression, stagnations, and suicidal thoughts will tremble and shake when they hear the roar of the lion come up out of you. When you give your life to the Lord and you begin to live a life of purification and justification, righteousness is imputed into you. In 1 Corinthians 3:16, Apostle Paul said, "Know ye not that ye are the temple of God, and that the Spirit of God dwelleth in you?" When you accept Jesus Christ as your Lord and Savior, he then lives in you, and because Jesus lives in you, the lion lives in you. Do you know why the lion lives in you? If you read Revelation 5:5, John, the revelator, references Jesus as the Lion of Judah, and we know that there is power in the name of Jesus. This is the reason you should not be fearful in this hour. The Lord did not give you the spirit of fear, but he has given you power, love, and a sound mind.

When I think of a lion, I surmise on *The Lion King* movie when the hyenas were attacking Simba and Nala. When Mufasa arrived on the scene, he roared so loud that the hyenas ran away from the children. In that scene, there was a shaking in that environment, and you need to understand that when you give God a loud cry, you will cause every trauma and triggers of the devil to shake and be dismantled because you were able to become bold in faith. I do not care what issues you may face right now. You will not be bound forever.

The word of God in your mouth will dismantle every chain that has you locked up.

Apostle Paul and Silas were in prison, and the Scripture says that when it was midnight, Paul and Silas prayed and sang praises unto the Lord. The Lord answered their cry by shaking the foundation of the jailhouse, and he freed everyone who was bound with chains (see Acts 16:16–26). Your mouth is a weapon of praise and power. This is the benefit of being righteous. Yes, the Bible says "Ask and you shall receive," but you can go beyond the asking and be bold in the face of the enemy because Job said, "Thou shalt decree a thing, and it shall be established" (Job 22:28 KJV).

Everything is going to come back not because God said so, but because you said so. According to your faith, all things will work together for the good because you are not afraid to open your mouth and declare the word of the Lord. Declare that over your life and say "never bound!" You will never be bound because Jesus broke every chain, and it is because you were not afraid to cry aloud. Because Jesus lives, you will be able to face tomorrow. Because Jesus lives in you, you do not have to be fearful. Be strong in the Lord. Do not be afraid to use your mouth. To see the manifestation of God moving in your life, open your mouth wide open and give God a loud cry so that your enemies can hear you. Be the voice that God called you to be in all your circumstances. Speak the word of the Lord over your life, and you will gain the victory in Jesus's name!

CHAPTER 5

REACHING THE FINISH LINE

Now that you have all the tools and the knowledge about the power of the mouth as a spiritual weapon, you are ready to enter into the race. The purpose of being in this race is to become prosperous and to gain the victory. Throughout your Christian journey, you are in a race. Unlike an athletic race competition you see in colleges and high schools that would last for a night or for a season, this Christian race will last for a lifetime. The race will be over at the point of death, but if there is available life, then the race will continue. It is up to you to win every race until it is time that the Lord sees your faithfulness and that you are called to be with him in eternal glory. The race that you will embark on is not going to be placid, but the Lord wants you to finish well and strong. Stumbling on roadblocks or spiritual failures can result in the race not being completed fully, but the Lord made a promise to never leave you. It is recommended best to put God in your life, in everything that you do, and in everything that you go through. Without God, you can't do anything.

In Acts 17:28, Apostle Paul states, "For in him we live, and move, and have our being." Have God be in the race with you. If you don't have the strength of God with you, how are you going to finish strong? God puts us in the race for a reason. Hebrews 12:1 states, "Wherefore seeing we also are compassed about with so great a cloud of witnesses, and let us lay aside every weight, and the sin which doth so easily beset us, and let us run with patience the race that is set before us." When the author mentions the word *witnesses*, those who ran in the Old Testament victoriously were referred to as the witnesses.

This spiritual race is not something to jape with or make a mockery of, but it is the real deal. The race is a battleground, not a playground. The Christian battle is intended for true soldiers of Jesus Christ, and the main goal is to win the fight against our enemies. We will then expose the devil's true colors. What are the devil's true colors? Yes, you guessed right! The devil is manipulative, sneaky, and a pathological liar. It is imperative that all should learn about fierce perseverance and endurance. Perseverance is defined as the persistence in doing something despite the hardship of executing great success. Endurance is the power of enduring pain—whether physical, mental, or emotional—without the use of giving up.

God is not the god of temptation. He will not put you in a position of suffering to punish you, but rather build and equip you to become stronger. In order for a Christian to become stronger and more mature, they must go through the fire. God sees you as a good soldier, and if you want to be acknowledged by God as a good soldier, then you must endure hardship. You can be encouraged by the Word of God to know how to finish well in the battlefield. The way to gain endurance and encouragement is to examine the Old Testament's godly leaders and how they endured the race with confidence.

While facing hardship, embrace the love of God and hope. The apostle Paul said, "There hath no temptation taken you but such as is common to man: but God is faithful, who will not suffer you to be tempted above that ye are able; but will with the temptation also make a way to escape, that ye may be able to bear it" (1 Corinthians 10:13 KJV). The strength of God will help you to endure, and his hand of love is always around us at the dimension of suffering. Faith in Jesus and having the endurance will definitely pay off. Embracing hope will enlarge our growth in God and will bring us closer to him, which will cause us to not be weary. The apostle Paul stated in Galatians 6:9 "to not be weary in well doing, but in due season we shall reap if we faint not."

Remember in one of the chapters, we talked about not giving in to the devil's plans? While you are in this race, it is imperative not to give in. Being in this race is not easy, but with the help of the Lord, you can conquer all. In this Christian journey, we suffer because we encounter greater faith and greater hope. God inducts you in the race, but it depends upon you. The life of a Christian is a difficult life because we will encounter spiritual warfare. You're positioned in the race, and there is no first place in the race. Don't let anyone compromise your position in Christ while you're enduring the pain and in this spiritual battle.

When soldiers are in the army, they prepare themselves. They sometimes polish their equipment to be equipped for war. Most importantly, they endure. Good Christian soldiers should always be prepared for battle. To be fully prepared, every Christian should carry the armor of God. According to Ephesians 6:10–18, the apostle Paul gives the people of God the necessary tools that make up the full armor of God. Verse 11 says, "Put on the whole armor of God, that ye may be able to stand against the wiles of the devil." When you are fully armed, no weapon that the enemy will possess against you shall prosper. The book of Ephesians teaches us that the devil is a sneaky liar and desires us to hurt the ones we love and the heart of God. We shouldn't be fearful because, even though the devil is strong, the armor of God is stronger, which is given to us by the Holy Ghost. Let's examine the full armor of God:

(1) *The Belt of Truth.* The belt of truth holds everything together. Make sure that the belt is secured and tight. The truth is important in our battle because Satan is the master of telling lies. In the garden of Eden, he transformed himself as a snake and whispered lies to Eve, concerning the tree that God forbid Adam and Eve to go to. Today, Satan still whispers lies. However, the truth of God will protect us from his lies. The belt is a reminder to believe in the report of the Lord and to believe his faithful promises.

(2) *The Breastplate of Righteousness.* This tool covers our heart because Satan wants us to have an embarrassing experience in life due to our past sinful nature. He wants us to be separated from the love of God and to have a stony, cruel heart. When

our heart is pure, we are forgiven by the heart of God and by having the heart of righteousness to do right over wrong.

(3) *The Shoes of the Gospel of Peace.* Satan and his army buddies love being in the battle against the people of God. He wants us to become fearful and either slip or fall, but God wants us to stand strong in the shoes of the gospel. Satan tries to steal the peace of God from us and wants us to slip in the ground, but the gospel of Jesus Christ is powerful. The good news of Jesus Christ teaches us that no ground is too dangerous for God's soldiers to walk on. The love of God will place our feet on solid ground. The shoes help us to remain solid and strong.

(4) *The Shield of Faith.* One of Satan's most deadly weapons is his mouth of words. Ephesians 6:16 describes Satan's words as fiery darts. One word from his mouth can cause a flame of fire to transpire in your heart with fear and worry. The shield of faith blocks every dart that the devil throws at us. Faith in the Lord is a powerful weapon, and because our faith is in Jesus, our faith is stronger. Jesus is everything! He is the greatest of kings, he is our reigning champion, and Jesus dismantles every weapon from our enemies.

(5) *The Helmet of Salvation.* The human mind is imperative in the body because it is used to help us surmise on certain areas in our lives. Satan wants to fill our minds with information that's not true and not legit. God has given us the helmet of salvation to protect our minds. It covers our minds and the truth of God. It is important to fill our minds with the thoughts and ways of God.

(6) *The Sword of the Spirit.* This is a mighty weapon that soldiers of God must use. The apostle Paul references the sword of the spirit as the word of God. This is the first weapon that Satan *can't* fight against. There is no other weapon like it. This amazing, powerful weapon teaches the soldiers of God how to fight, and it leads us into the future. Satan is frightened by this future because the end of God's Word reveals that God will defeat Satan.

When you put on the whole armor of God, you are putting on Jesus. In order to put on Jesus, you have to know him. Now that you are guarded with the full armor of God, you shouldn't be fearful of the tactics of the enemy. When you begin to put on the armor of God and you submit yourself unto the Lord, the devil is forced to vanish away from you and your life. James said, "Submit yourselves therefore unto God. Resist the devil, and he will flee from you" (James 4:7). You are in this race, and there is no turning back. Don't let Satan put fear inside you while running this race. You're close to the finish line. Keep on moving forward. In Philippians 3:13–14, the apostle Paul states, "Brethren, I count not myself to have apprehended: but this one thing I do, forgetting those things which are behind, and reaching forth unto those things which are before. I press toward the mark for the prize of the high calling of God in Christ Jesus." Forget about the past and keep on pressing toward your destiny.

Take a look at this story example. A sailor is sailing from one end of the sea to the Bahamas. The Bahama Islands is his final mark. He tried sailing to the island before, but every time he sails, something goes wrong during the trip. As the man is peddling his boat up toward the island, he then sees crocodiles on each side, which are preventing him from making it to the finish line. This time, the sailor makes a determination to push himself to make his final arrival. He uses his paddle sticks to push the crocodiles out of the way, and instantly, he is in the Bahamas.

To conclude this chapter, I want you to understand that whatever you need to do to get to your finish line, do just that. If you have to run, then run. If you have to walk, then walk. If you have to speed walk, then speed walk. If you have to jump, then jump. If you have to crawl, then crawl. Destiny can't stop here. Declare this word with confidence over your own life and say, "Destiny can't stop here."

When I was growing up in my family church, one of our late church mothers by the name of Mother Alice Clark would sing the song "I'm Pressing on the Upward Way." You are gaining new heights every day. Keep on pushing beyond the pain, the frustration, and the doubt. Continue praying and having strong faith in the Lord. Instead of saying "I quit," "I give up," or "I can't do this anymore,"

I want you to say "I can," "I will," and "I will conquer." You are able to do all things through Christ because he gives you the strength to do so. You will reach the finish line, and when you do, you will be victorious. We will fight, we will win, and we shall decree victory in the name of the Lord Jesus Christ over our lives!

CHAPTER 6

IT'S TIME TO REJOICE

Now THAT YOU HAVE the armor of God with you and you are purpose-driven, you are ready to cross over into your destiny. The race wasn't an easy race. You wanted to quit, give up, and even throw in the towel, but you held on to God's unchanging hand. With the strength of God, you were able to endure the pain and conquer this fight. You have won this battle. You didn't run this race alone, but you had Yahweh with you. This is one of the advantages of living as a child of God. Every circumstance that you're in, you will not be in it alone. Family, friends, or coworkers will walk away from you, but the promises of God never fail. You have won the race, broken the tape, and now it is time to have a praise party. Because of your faith, dedication, determination, and confidence in the race, you were able to prove the devil wrong. He concluded you as being weak, but you are made strong. Now you can ask Satan, "Where is your victory now?" Be bold and look at the face of Satan with an L in front of your forehead to show him that he is a *loser*!

What the devil has plotted to take you out or to kill you, his plans were expunged because you have total victory written on you. Your name is *victory*, and your purpose is to be victorious. The apostle Paul said to always rejoice in the Lord. Read Philippians 4:4; *rejoice* simply means to express joy or to be glad. A child of God should always rejoice in the Lord, both in the good times and the bad times. If you have a genuine relationship with God, then you should always rejoice. Because of Jesus Christ, the relationship with God is much

32

stronger, and that is something to rejoice about. There are a lot of reasons it is a great feeling to rejoice during trials, triggers, and traumas. The afflictions that the righteous face are only temporary. The apostle Paul stated, "Our present troubles are small and won't last very long" (2 Corinthians 4:17 NLT). Don't give up or become distressed. Be anchored in Jesus, and know that what you face will only last temporality because when the Lord gets ready, he will deliver you out of all the afflictions you encounter.

Another reason to rejoice during trauma is knowing that everything will be for your good. According to Romans 5:3–4, Paul lets us know that our trouble and pain helps to strengthen our endurance and character. The benefit of our character is a reward for favor from the Lord. One of the reasons the devil likes to throw darts at the people of God is because he wants to steal our joy away from us. Don't let the devil steal your joy. Whenever you handle trouble, it is your opportunity to have great joy because endurance has a chance to grow and be strengthened, with the help of the Lord. The apostle James said, "Dear brothers and sisters, when trouble of any kind, consider it an opportunity for great joy. For you know that when your faith is tested, your endurance has a chance to grow" (James 1:2–3). Remember chapter 5 about endurance? If you go back to that chapter, you will see that the Lord helps you to bear the pain and the suffering. This is why you can have great joy and rejoice because you know that you are never alone. Your marriage will not die, your family will not be lost, and you will not bear the physical pain alone because the Lord is always with you.

I love teaching the Word of God to my Bible group, and whenever I am in the hospital to treat my sickle cell pain crisis, my group members always say to me, "How are you able to teach when you're in a lot of pain?" My response to them is this: "The Lord's got me covered. He is always with me." Yes, I cry, and I ask the Lord about my sickness. I asked the Lord about the pain in my wounds, but the Lord revealed to me two years ago that my healing is on the way. This is why I can rejoice because the god I serve got me. I can say, "Hallelujah, I am not alone!"

Another reason to rejoice is because the joy of the Lord is your strength. Nehemiah 8:10 says, "Don't be dejected and sad, for the joy of the Lord is your strength!" You shouldn't faint or become weak if you carry the strength of the Lord. The last reason to rejoice is because you are preparing yourself for a turnaround. Declare that declaration over your life and say, "My family and I will experience a turnaround in the name of Jesus!" There will be a change that will begin to manifest, and while you wait for the turnaround, keep on rejoicing. Don't let anyone stop you from praising God. Don't allow the devil to keep you quiet. Roar like a lion, and break out in a praise. This is the genesis for you—that a change will take place in your life. Be ready and in position for restoration and renewal.

CHAPTER 7

PRAYERS OF COMFORT AND VICTORY

THE LORD LED ME to do this chapter to pray over everything that you may be dealing with. Some of you might be dealing with depression, anxiety, abandonment of friends and family, sickness, or you might want to give your life over to the Lord. These are my words of prayers, but I want you to recite these prayers in your heart and believe in God. My prayer is for you to reach your mark and be prosperous. My grandparents and parents taught me well how to pray. My mom always says to me, "Don't be discouraged, and just talk to the Lord." A great brother of mine, who is an elder from North Carolina, said to me, "Stop and pray." Whenever I think about both my mother's statement and the elder's statement on prayer, I think about elementary school when the students visit the firefighter's station, and the firefighters say that whenever you see a fire, do this: stop, drop, and roll. I say this to all my readers. Whenever you encounter great trials and traumas, don't panic, but stop, drop on your knees at the throne of God, and pray to your heavenly Father.

1. This prayer is for marriages and relationships:
    Father God, in the name of Jesus. Lord, we are thankful that you have united us together. We are having issues in our marriage and our relationship. We see that the devil is tearing us apart. We ask that you restore our marriage and bring us back to a level of peace. Lord, bring us together in unity and in love. Comfort us and wrap your loving arms

around us. Direct us, God, so that we will have a healthy marriage. Strengthen our communication, Lord. Allow us to talk to each other and not at each other. Lead us and guide us along the way so that our marriage will be prosperous. We speak restoration in the name of Jesus. We ask that you heal our marriage, O God. We are trusting in you and depending on you, Lord. All these things we ask in the name of Jesus. Amen.

2.   This prayer is for healing of the body:

Father God, in the name of Jesus. Lord, we believe that we are healed by your stripes, and we decree healing to our bodies in the name of Jesus. Heal us from the top of our heads to the soles of our feet. Devil, we are not asking you to leave our bodies, but we are *telling* you to. This body doesn't belong to you; this body belongs to the Lord. We speak manifestation now in the name of Jesus. We decree and believe that it is so. Let it be done according to our faith. We are healed in the name of Jesus! Amen.

3.   This prayer is for those who felt abandoned and who suffered mental, emotional pain and depression:

Father God, in the name of Jesus. God, I ask that you to comfort me during this time of abandonment. Lord, I have family members and friends who abandoned me and made me feel like I was worthless. It caused me to be depressed and to become an outcast, away from the crowd. Lord, help me to realize that I am better with you. God, you are father to the fatherless, a mother to the motherless, and a friend to the friendless. I am considered your friend, and I thank you for comforting me. Thank you for not leaving me. Thank you for always sticking with me.

God, I dismantle the spirit of depression now in the name of Jesus. This spirit can't have me anymore, but I shall obtain the joy of the Lord because the joy of the Lord is my strength. God, I ask that you heal every brokenness and anger. Cut out any bitterness and wrath that's in me. Anything that is not like you, please purge me right now.

Instill in me a new heart, and replace the stony heart away so that I can walk in your statutes and keep on following your commandments. Strengthen my love for you so that I may have the heart to love and the heart to forgive those who backstabbed me, criticized me, and belittled me.

Change me, O God. Make me more like you, Jesus. I want to be refreshed and renewed in the name of Jesus. Wipe all the tears of sadness and discouragement off my eyes, and allow the tears of joy to flow down my face. You said in your word that blessed are the pure in heart for they shall see God. Lord, I want to see your face, and I want to be with you, Lord. Clean my hands and purify my heart, Lord. Restore my heart, my mind, and my soul. Do it for me, God. I believe that according to my faith, it is so. In the name of Jesus, I pray. Amen!

4. This prayer is for salvation and deliverance:

If you desire to be saved and have a genuine relationship with the Lord, then this is your moment. The Bible says in Acts 2:21 (KJV), "And it shall come to pass, that whosoever shall call on the name of the Lord shall be saved." If you've been saved before but you strayed away from God and you want to stay on course with God, then I want you to recite this word of prayer. Say it, and believe in the Lord Jesus Christ.

Father God, in the name of Jesus. I have made mistakes, and I have done the wrong things. I have sinned, but today, I am beginning a new path. Today, I want to be saved. Lord Jesus, I ask that you forgive me from all my sins. Wash me, and make me whole. I confess with my mouth and that I believe in my heart that God raised his son, Jesus, to die on the cross for me. Thank you, Jesus, for forgiving me, loving me, receiving me, and accepting me. Fill me with your Holy Spirit. Lead me into the path of righteousness, and I will never be the same. For the rest of my life, I will serve the Lord. Jesus is my Lord and savior, and I belong to him. Amen!

If you prayed that prayer and you believe wholeheartedly that Jesus saved you, I, the author of this great book, want to welcome you to the family of God. Those who have accepted Jesus and are saved, I will be interceding and go in prayer for you so that you will be guided in the right path. Just know that nothing can separate you from the love of God.

ACKNOWLEDGMENTS

I WANT TO THANK EVERYONE for reading this book. I pray that you allow this book to become a learning tool on how to be a dangerous force to the devil and how to be prosperous—whether marriage or relationship is restored, family is restored and at peace, a new employment, casting down depression, or even in renewing a relationship with the Lord. My goal was for you to be victorious and to reach your destiny. I know how it feels when you want to pursue another dimension, but there are roadblocks preventing you from moving forward. I became depressed and hurt, but the Lord led me in 2018 to write this book for you and for me to turn my pain into a product. To all my great readers, you will be in my prayers.

I want to thank my grandparents, the late apostle Willie Lee Maxwell and the late missionary mother Nancy Maxwell, for praying for and with me. I thank God for making them become true examples of bold soldiers with faith. I thank them for teaching me about faith and to have a relationship with the Lord. I received the Lord at the age of sixteen, and I'm not turning back. I love you, Grandma and Papa, and I miss you. You will be forever in my heart.

To my grandma McCaskill, I want to say thank you for your encouraging words and for persuading me not to give up, but to have faith in the Lord and to work hard.

To my loving parents, thank you for being in my life and for always pushing me to pray to the Lord while being in the midst of my circumstances. Thank you for your support, your love, and your prayers. I love you so very much.

To my family and close friends, thank you for pushing me, supporting me, encouraging me, and loving me. I love you!

ABOUT THE AUTHOR

 Navoun Maxwell is a native of Hackensack, New Jersey. He is a proud son to Latiesha McCaskill and Robert McCaskill Sr. He is a counseling graduate student at Grand Canyon University. Navoun is a proud and faithful member of the Latter Glory Church, under the tutelage of Apostle Derrick Etienne Sr. and Lady Shamone Etienne. Navoun has a heart and passion of helping individuals to move forward and to have a successful life. He sees potential in everyone and is willing to help them push toward their prophetic purpose and season with the help of the Lord.

CPSIA information can be obtained
at www.ICGtesting.com
Printed in the USA
BVHW07055028I221
624941BV00002B/169

9 781639 032624